IN THE SHADOW
OF GOD'S WINGS

Grace in the Midst of Depression

GROUP STUDY GUIDE

IN THE SHADOW OF GOD'S WINGS

Grace in the Midst of Depression

GROUP STUDY GUIDE

SUSAN GREGG-SCHROEDER

UPPER ROOM BOOKS
NASHVILLE

IN THE SHADOW OF GOD'S WINGS
Grace in the Midst of Depression
GROUP STUDY GUIDE
© 1998 by Susan Gregg-Schroeder
All rights reserved.

The Upper Room Web Site: http://www.upperroom.org

Art Direction: Michele Wetherbee
Cover Design: Meg McWhinney
Cover Design (original book): Laura Beers
Cover Photograph (original book): © 1996 William Neill
        Photography
First printing 1998

Library of Congress Cataloging-in-Publication
Gregg-Schroeder, Susan, 1947–
        In the shadow of God's wings: group study guide / Susan
Gregg-Schroeder.
        p.   cm.
        Includes bibliographical references.
        ISBN 0-8358-0859-9 (pbk.)
        1. Gregg-Schroeder, Susan, 1947–   In the shadow of
God's wings. 2. Depression, Mental—Religious aspects—
Christianity. 3. Church work with the mentally ill. 4. Depressed
persons—United States—Case studies. 5. Gregg-Schroeder,
Susan, 1947–   I. Title.
BV4910.34.G743G74   1998
248.8" 8—dc21   98-16312
                                                                        CIP

Printed in the United States of America on acid-free paper

Contents

Introduction

DEPRESSION IS NOTORIOUSLY IMPARTIAL, striking even those whose professional training has prepared them to understand its insidious nature. In this remarkably candid work, Susan Gregg-Schroeder allows us to look deep within her soul as she learns to live with this illness, which is increasingly so much a part of our world. She openly shares not only her personal journey but that of her family as together they walk through depression's dark shadows.

Pastor of a large urban church, Gregg-Schroeder challenges the church to look at its understanding of mental illness. A survey done by the California Alliance for the Mentally Ill (CAMI) showed that although 40 percent of CAMI families sought the help of clergy when faced with mental illness, the families ranked clergy last in terms of their helpfulness and support. Seminary curriculum rarely incorporates information about mental illness. Depression continues to carry stigma and shame with it, and clergy and laity alike often view depression as a personal weakness or evidence of a lack of faith, rather than as a treatable illness.

At the heart of *In the Shadow of God's Wings* rests the assertion that God's grace not only helps us survive the darkness of the shadows but that out of these shadows we can find "gifts of the shadow." Gregg-Schroeder states that "dark nights of our soul—whether caused by illness, crisis, or some unknown origin—can be pathways to transformation and healing, opportunities for personal growth, and the means of becoming new persons in Christ" (page 62, *In the Shadow of God's Wings*).

The author discusses the importance of shared story. In telling her personal story, Gregg-Schroeder clearly communicates the "gifts" she discovered in her depression. These gifts include the gifts of vulnerability, the discovery of one's authentic self, patience within a process, living with paradox, creativity, and hope. The connection between the shadow and the spiritual gifts of the shadow makes this book a unique source of comfort and hope.

—THE EDITOR

Helps for Leaders

T HE INTENTION OF THIS STUDY GUIDE is to serve as a resource tool with a small-group adult study. The study guide provides the basis for four one and one-half hour sessions, although some groups may decide to meet for two hours. You also may adapt this guide to a weekend retreat setting. (See suggestions for a retreat schedule and additional options on page 15.)

FORMING A GROUP

Be sure the publicity states that the group is open both to persons who have personal experience with depression and to those who want to learn more about this illness. Since this study encourages participant discussion and mutual support, a commitment to attend all four sessions is helpful. Announce and confirm the time and place of the first meeting in writing. Encourage participants to be on time.

An effective group can have as few as four or five committed participants but certainly no more than twelve. You may choose to have separate groups for men and women in order to build trust and to open the way for sharing life experiences.

Each participant needs a copy of In the Shadow of God's Wings at least a week before the first session. At the time participants receive their books, give them a copy of the session study guides (pages 65–79 of this resource). You may copy all four guides and hand them out in their entirety, or you may distribute the study guides one session at a time. It helps the participants to have the study questions before them as they do the week's reading. Then they can reflect on the content as it applies to their lives. Also included for the participants' information is background material on depression. (See Materials for Group Distribution, page 41.)

It is preferable that one person facilitate the four sessions. The group leader is not a person who knows all the answers but rather a leader who can encourage the group participants to share experiences and feelings.

CREATING SACRED SPACE

Take care in preparing the group's meeting space. A quiet, comfortable room where chairs can be set in a circle is desirable. Nametags, which participants may reuse each session, are helpful, especially if the participants do not know one another. You may choose to have beverages and/or snack foods available at the end of each session.

Set up a "worship center" in the middle of the circle of chairs. This center may consist of something as simple as a small table covered with material and a meaningful object displayed. By lighting a candle to mark the beginning of the session, you encourage participants' punctuality and openness to the Spirit's leading.

Creating sacred space is more than the setting. The group leader can help create a safe place for all participants by establishing certain ground rules the first session:

- *Confidentiality*. Because of the sensitive nature of the study, group members need to protect each person's confidentiality. What persons say in the room stays in the room.

- *Respect for the rights of others*. The group also needs to respect each participant by listening nonjudgmentally and sensitively, by guaranteeing each person time to share, and by allowing persons the right to "pass" or not to participate in any exercise.

Some group members may want to be in touch with one another for support during the study. With the permission of the participants, the leader may provide a list of the group members and their phone numbers.

The leader can model and encourage openness and trust in the group by willingly sharing his or her thoughts. Taking the time to create a safe and sacred space will allow everyone to receive what he or she needs from this study.

USING THE DISCUSSION QUESTIONS

Pass out the study guide prior to each session. During this four-week study, encourage participants to keep a journal in which they record their feelings and thoughts. They may respond to the study questions or simply allow the questions to lead them in other directions.

Journaling can provide wonderful spiritual discipline. When writing in a journal, do not attempt to edit or judge what is written. Do not worry about correct spelling, grammar, or punctuation. The purpose of the journaling is to capture the feelings and thoughts of the moment as the Spirit leads.

As the leader, do not feel that you have to cover all the questions and suggested activities in this guide. Choose those that seem most important to the group. If participant discussion tends to focus on one question or if discussion moves on to an unrelated subject, gently guide the participants back to the topic by moving on to another question. For some of the more sensitive questions, you may wish to form smaller groups of two or three persons.

Quotations for Session Use

⁓

Everything that we see is a shadow cast by that which we do not see. (Martin Luther King Jr., *The Measure of Man*)

There is light in shadow, and shadow in light,
   and black in the blue of the sky.
(Lucy Larcom, 19th century)

Who has not come upon a season when the water of the soul is disturbed? And does not God meet each of us as we brave the swirling dark in search of wholeness? (Sue Monk Kidd)

If darkness is meant to convey a sense of uncertainty, of being lost, of being afraid; if darkness suggests conflict...then we live in a world that knows much about darkness. Darkness is what our newspapers are about. Darkness is what most of our contemporary literature is about....And in our single lives, we know much about darkness too. If we are people who pray, darkness is apt to be a lot of what our prayers are about. If we are people who do not pray, it is apt to be darkness in one form or another that has stopped our mouths. (Frederick Buechner, *The Hungering Dark*)

He brought light out of darkness, not out of lesser light. He can bring thy summer out of winter though thou have no spring. Though in the ways of fortune, or under-standing, or conscience, thou have been benighted till now, wintered and frozen, clouded and eclipsed, damped and benumbed, smothered and stupefied till now, now God comes to thee, not as the dawning of the day, not as in the bud of the spring, but as the sun at noon. (John Donne)

A Christian community is therefore a healing commu-nity not because wounds are cured and pains are allevi-ated, but because wounds and pains become openings or occasions for a new vision. (Henri J. M. Nouwen, *The Wounded Healer*)

"Hope" is the thing with feathers—
That perches in the soul—
And sings the tune without the words—
And never stops—at all— (Emily Dickinson)

Suggestions for a Weekend Retreat

⟪⟫

SUGGESTED SCHEDULE

Friday Night

7:00 P.M.	Gathering and welcoming
7:30–9:00	Session 1
9:00–9:30	Explain Covenant Group concept; Covenant Groups meet for introductions
9:30–10:00	Social time

Saturday

7:45 A.M.	Morning prayer
8:00–9:00	Breakfast
9:00–10:30	(See "An Experiential Session for a Weekend Retreat")
10:30–10:45	Break
10:45–11:30	Meet in Covenant Groups
11:30–12:00	Free time
12:00 P.M.	Lunch
1:00–4:00	Free time (1:00–2:00 is silent time)
4:00–5:00	Session 2
5:00–5:45	Meet in Covenant Groups
5:45–6:00	Free time
6:00–7:00	Dinner
7:00–8:00	Session 3 (*Option A*)

	(*Option B*: videotape—"Gifts in the Shadows"—see resource list)
8:00–9:00	Skits with Covenant Groups
9:00	Social time

Sunday

7:45 A.M.	Morning Prayer
8:00–9:00	Breakfast
9:00–10:00	Session 4
10:00–10:45	Meet in Covenant Groups
10:45–11:00	Free time
11:00–12:00	Worship
12:00	Lunch and departure

AN EXPERIENTIAL SESSION FOR A WEEKEND RETREAT

In his book *Transforming Depression—Healing the Soul through Creativity*, David H. Rosen shows that when people learn to explore the rich images and symbols that emerge from their struggles, they can turn their despair into a fountain of creative energy. This session will encourage us to "become as little children." A group size of thirty to forty persons is optimum for a weekend retreat.

After listening to the guided meditation tape selection "Healing Special Memory" (from the audiocassette *Depth Healing and Renewal through Christ: Guided Meditations for Inner Healing*, written and read by Flora Slosson Wuellner, Upper Room Books), allow participants to express whatever emerges from the guided meditation through a variety of creative mediums.

This meditation is really a form of active imagination, and participants may use it as a vehicle for opening themselves to feelings, images, symbols or whatever appears as they recall a dark time in their lives or an unhealed memory.

~ 16 ~

Darken the room and allow participants to make themselves comfortable either in their chairs or lying on the floor, if possible. After listening to the meditation, participants will have a half hour to create a mandala, using a variety of art materials (clay, colored pens, crayons, etc.).

Mandalas are circular designs that symbolize the self, healing, and wholeness. Throughout the ages and in all parts of the world, people have created mandalas as acts of worship, as prayers for healing, and as a way of bringing harmony to inner conflict. *In the Shadow of God's Wings* emerged from such an experience at a retreat center. (Refer to pages 93–94, *In the Shadow of God's Wings.*)

After the creative art experience, give group members an opportunity to share what emerged for them.

THE USE OF COVENANT GROUPS

Covenant groups, smaller groups of no more than five or six persons within a larger retreat setting, allow participants to process the material and their own feelings in a safe, small group. Each person is encouraged to listen, care, and share his or her respective journey.

The leader assigns retreatants to groups before the weekend, designating one person in each group as the facilitator. The facilitator can help ensure the group's effectiveness by setting the ground rules and principles of community building, trust, and confidentiality.

The covenant groups will meet four times throughout the weekend. An openness to the workings and movings of the Spirit is vital to each group's discovery and growth in its unique way.

Additional Resources for Leaders

VIDEOTAPES

Videotapes for the *Midpoint* series shown nationally on the Odyssey Cable Network.

Depression #404 (with Rev. Gregg-Schroeder)
Teenage Depression #501
Adult Depression #502
Gifts in the Shadows #503 (with Rev. Gregg-Schroeder)

Available from Pacific Media Ministry
1775 Hancock Street, Suite 200
San Diego, CA 92110-2036
800-883-4897

AUDIOCASSETTE TAPES

Depth Healing and Renewal through Christ: Guided Meditations for Inner Healing
Written and read by Flora Slosson Wuellner
Available through Upper Room Books
800-972-0433

BOOKS

Bohler, Carolyn Stahl. *Opening to God: Guided Imagery Meditation on Scripture*. Nashville: Upper Room Books, 1996. Bohler offers fifty guided meditations for use by individuals or groups.

Broyles, Anne. *Journaling: A Spirit Journey.* Nashville: Upper Room Books, 1988. Journaling as a spiritual discipline is presented through six approaches: from daily life events, in response to scripture, with guided meditations, from dreams, in response to quotations, and as conversations or dialogues.

Buechner, Frederick. *Telling Secrets.* San Francisco: HarperSanFrancisco, 1992. Buechner tells how keeping secrets may wound a life, and how the telling of secrets can bring healing and wholeness.

Buechner, Frederick. *The Sacred Journey: A Memoir of Early Days.* San Francisco: HarperSanFrancisco, 1991. Buechner's spiritual memoir of childhood, adolescence, and young adulthood.

Cameron, Julia. *The Artist's Way: A Spiritual Path to Higher Creativity.* New York: The Putnam Publishing Group, 1992. This book contains a twelve-week program to recover creativity from a variety of blocks, including limiting beliefs, fear, self-sabotage, jealousy, guilt, addictions, and other inhibiting forces, replacing them with artistic confidence and productivity. Cameron also links creativity to our spirituality.

Kelsey, Morton T. *Adventure Within: Christian Growth through Personal Journal Writing.* Minneapolis, Minn.: Augsburg Fortress Publishers, 1980. Kelsey provides a step-by-step introduction to the use of journaling as a spiritual discipline.

Kidd, Sue Monk. *When the Heart Waits: Spiritual Direction for Life's Sacred Questions.* San Francisco: HarperSanFrancisco,

1991. Sue Monk Kidd, a spiritual pilgrim, allows the reader to accompany her as she delves deeply and personally into the sacred questions and struggles of midlife.

May, Gerald G. *Addiction and Grace: Love and Spirituality in the Healing of Addiction*. San Francisco: HarperSanFrancisco, 1991. According to May, we are all addicted—not just to substance abuse but to beliefs, relationships, habits, and almost any dimension of behavior. Our only hope for freedom is divine grace.

Moore, Thomas. *Care of the Soul: A Guide for Cultivating Depth and Sacredness in Everyday Life*. New York: HarperCollins, 1992. This unique book combines Moore's training in theology with that of psychology. In understanding psychology and spirituality as one, he offers insights that bring together the mind, body, spirit connection.

Nouwen, Henri J. M. *The Wounded Healer: Ministry in Contemporary Society*. New York: Doubleday, 1979. Nouwen calls suffering persons to make their suffering and pain the starting point of their service to others. Church leaders need to allow themselves to be open to others as fellow human beings with the same wounds and hurts.Palmer, Parker J. *The Active Life: Wisdom for Work, Creativity, and Caring*. San Francisco: HarperSanFrancisco, 1991. Using material from diverse traditions, Palmer shares a way of living that unites contemplation and action.

Sanford, John A. *The Kingdom Within: The Inner Meaning of Jesus' Sayings*. San Francisco: HarperSanFrancisco, 1987. This book acknowledges our inner world as a spiritual reality in order to develop a creative, personal relationship with God.

Styron, William. *Darkness Visible: A Memoir of Madness*. New York: Random House, 1990. Styron describes his descent into a crippling and almost suicidal depression.

Wuellner, Flora Slosson. *Heart of Healing, Heart of Light: Encountering God, Who Shares and Heals Our Pain*. Nashville: Upper Room Books, 1992. This book is a warm invitation to search and discover the heart and love of God that can heal our personal pains.

Wuellner, Flora Slosson. *Release: Healing from Wounds of Family, Church, and Community*. Nashville: Upper Room Books, 1996. This book offers hope to persons dealing with emotional scars caused by family or generational pain or by church or community distress. Wuellner uses Bible passages, scripture-based meditations, and prayer to help deal with unhealed wounds.

Session 1
Understanding Depression

Before the session, read the Prologue and chapter 1 of *In the Shadow of God's Wings*.

SESSION OBJECTIVES

- To understand the importance of shared story
- To explore the feelings and images associated with shadow

SESSION MATERIALS

- Copies of *In the Shadow of God's Wings* for anyone who previously has not received one
- Extra copies of the discussion questions
- Small table and candle for worship center
- Box of tissues
- Sheets of construction paper in a variety of colors
- Basket for the construction paper scraps
- Copies of the discussion guide for Session 2 if not distributed already

OPENING

Invite participants to center quietly for a few moments as you light the candle. You or a person you have asked in advance may share a prayer or poem.

Instruct members to choose a sheet of colored construction paper. Ask them to tear the paper into a shape that represents their life at this time. Then go around the circle, permitting each participant to introduce himself or herself by name and to share the significance of the color chosen and the shape he or she has torn.

After completing the introductions, collect the shapes and tape them to the wall or poster board to make a collage. Ask a volunteer to collect all the scrap paper in a basket. Place the basket on or near the worship center. Finish the exercise by reminding participants that their lives are made up *both* of the image they have of themselves as well as the scraps that are collected in the basket. Allow silent time for reflection, and then move into sharing about the experience as the members are willing to respond.

QUESTIONS FOR GROUP REFLECTION

1. "Story has great power, transforming power. Part of that transforming power comes from the intimacy of storytelling. The stories of our faith heritage, the stories of others, and our own stories make up the fabric of our soul" (page 11, *In the Shadow of God's Wings*).

When have hearing another's story or sharing your own story "become windows through which we look at the experiences that have shaped our lives and the lives of others?" (page 11, *In the Shadow of God's Wings*)

2. What happens when we keep family secrets, when we do not share our stories because of shame, guilt, or fear of others' reactions?

3. What words or images come to mind when you think of the word *shadow*?

4. Recall a time in your life, past or present, when you have entered into deep darkness or the "valley of the shadow of death." How did you feel? How did others feel toward you? (Consider initiating a creative art experience where participants draw their feelings.)

LOOKING AHEAD

After confirming the time and place of the next meeting, be sure that all participants have a copy of the Session 2 Study Guide. Ask them to read chapters 2 and 3 of *In the Shadow of God's Wings*.

Encourage participants to keep a journal or to write notes on the study questions for these four weeks. Invite them to practice the discipline of journaling by recording their thoughts, feelings, struggles, hopes, and other concerns prompted by group discussion or by the reading of the book. For those inexperienced with journaling, suggest possible journal entries they might make, such as the following:

- Insights or questions arising from their reading

- Quotations from the book that have personal significance

- Reflections on how ideas in the book relate to their personal experience

- Thoughts, ideas, or questions that arise during group discussion

CLOSING

Ask participants to state aloud any prayer requests they would like group members to lift up during the coming week. Give time to share joys and concerns.

You may close by praying the following prayer found on pages 54–55 of *In the Shadow of God's Wings*.

Here I am, Divine Spirit,
*   living in the center of mystery.*
I catch glimpses of brilliant light
*   breaking in all around.*
Yet I am attracted to the darkness
*   that shields me*
*   that hides me*
*   that keeps me safe.*
I feel yearnings to birth
*   the creative spirit within.*
Yet I fear the changes
*   that new life will bring.*

It's hard to understand this place,
*   this center of mystery.*
The light and dark intermingle.
Life and death abide side by side.
It is here that I live the questions
*   in my soul,*
*   knowing that one day*
*   answers to those questions*
*   will be birthed*
*   from this center of mystery.*

Session 2
Caring for the Depressed Person

Read chapters 2 and 3 of *In the Shadow of God's Wings.*

SESSION OBJECTIVES

*   To recognize how grace works in our lives
*   To explore our understanding of suffering and how God is present in times of pain
*   To understand possible feelings, emotions, and actions that may accompany depression
*   To discover helpful ways to be with a person who is depressed

SESSION MATERIALS

*   Extra copies of discussion questions
*   Small table and candle for worship center
*   Box of tissues
*   Newsprint and felt-tip marker or chalkboard and chalk

OPENING

On a large piece of newsprint or chalkboard write the word *grace*. Ask participants to share their definitions of grace aloud. As they do, write the main descriptive words or phrases on the newsprint or chalkboard. After everyone has been given a chance to share, challenge the group members to develop a definition of grace with which all can agree. Record that definition.

QUESTIONS FOR REFLECTION

1. Western society often views suffering as the opposite of health. Westerners are strongly influenced by a form of early Christianity that saw evil in suffering. This form of Christianity understood suffering as shameful, something to be endured alone. Particularly before the nineteenth century, many Christians viewed suffering as punishment from God. Thus our society has come to value strength, health, and self-sufficiency. Fortunately this view of suffering is giving way to a more wholistic attitude. But many people still feel personally responsible for their suffering.

Why do you feel that people suffer?

2. The book relates the journey through depression as similar to experiencing the stages in the grief process: denial, isolation, anger, bargaining, depression, and acceptance.

As you recall your times of deep pain or depression, how do you identify with this process?

3. Depression affects relationship dynamics within the family and among friends. Often the caregiver becomes the one in need of care from others.

How does it feel to be in need of help? Are you able to ask for help from others in your times of physical, emotional, or psychological need? If not, what holds you back from asking for help?

4. When persons experience depression, they are often very hard on themselves for not being able to "snap out of it."

What might family and friends say or do that would be hurtful to someone who is depressed? In what ways can family and friends be helpful?

5. We are often quick to judge another's behavior when we have not been there ourselves. Parker J. Palmer, in his book *The Active Life*, writes, "In the midst of my depression I had a friend who took a different tack. Every afternoon at around four o'clock he came to me, sat in a chair, removed my shoes, and massaged my feet. He hardly said a word, but he was there, he was with me. He was a lifeline for me, a link to the human community and thus to my own humanity. He had no need to 'fix' me. He knew the meaning of compassion."

Knowing more about the illness of depression, how might you respond to a person suffering with depression?

6. The book relates the story of Elijah's experience with depression (pages 40–42, *In the Shadow of God's Wings;* and see 1 Kings 18–19). What does this story say about ways the faith community could respond to persons suffering with depression?

7. The story is told of discovering the bumper sticker with the words *Grace Happens* (page 49, *In the Shadow of God's Wings*). As you reflect on your life, when has God's grace surprised you?

Looking Ahead

Ask the group members to read chapter 4 of *In the Shadow of God's Wings*. Encourage them to keep writing in their journals and recording any thoughts or feelings that come up in their reading or from the group discussion.

CLOSING

You may close by praying the following prayer found on page 47 of *In the Shadow of God's Wings*.

Break into my confusion, God.
   Help me to know who I am
      and what I am meant to be.

Guide, uphold, and strengthen me,
   as I leave behind
   the world of limits and labels.

Guide, uphold and strengthen me,
   as together we create
   a world of infinite possibility.

Session 3

Discovering the Spiritual Gifts of Depression

R ead chapter 4 of *In the Shadow of God's Wings*.

SESSION OBJECTIVES

- To discover that periods of deep pain can, in time, yield spiritual gifts

- To explore the six gifts discussed in the book

- To understand that all of life involves change and that change and transition can be opportunities for a new beginning

SESSION MATERIALS

- Extra copies of discussion questions
- Small table and candle for worship center
- Box of tissue
- One votive candle for each participant
- Four Bibles for small group exercise

OPENING

After everyone is seated, turn off the lights and light the center candle on the worship center to symbolize the light of

Christ. Read the prayer by Thomas Merton (page 61, *In the Shadow of God's Wings*). Invite each participant to come forward and light one of the votive candles on the worship center. Each may share a prayer request with the group or in silence. After everyone has lit a votive candle, read the last two lines of the prayer. "I will trust you always though I may seem to be lost and in the shadow of death. I will not fear, for you are ever with me, and you will never leave me to face my perils alone." Invite the participants' awareness of the light in the darkness. After a period of silence, turn on the lights and proceed with the discussion questions. The candles may remain lit until the closing.

QUESTIONS FOR GROUP REFLECTION

1. A time of crisis can be an opportunity for personal and spiritual growth. Thomas Moore states in his book *Care of the Soul*, "If we persist in our modern way of treating depression as an illness to be cured only mechanically and chemically we may lose the gifts of soul that only depression can provide" (pages 59–60, *In the Shadow of God's Wings*).

Reflect on a difficult time in your life. What "gifts" did you receive from going through that time of darkness and sadness?

2. Henri J. M. Nouwen has written in his book *The Wounded Healer*, "A Christian community is therefore a healing community not because wounds are cured and pains are alleviated, but because wounds and pains become openings or occasions for a new vision" (page 94).

In the Shadow of God's Wings discusses three aspects of the gift of vulnerability: vulnerability to God, vulnerability to ourselves, and vulnerability to community. In what ways might our wounds become signs of hope and "occasions for a new vision" when we take a risk and share them?

3. Discovering the gift of one's authentic self requires discovering who you are as a child of God. This discovery can be a lifelong process. What are some ways that you honor yourself so as to discover the treasure hidden in the field of your soul?

4. A Russian proverb says, "The future belongs to those who know how to wait." Waiting can be a time of emptiness. Sue Monk Kidd, in her book *When the Heart Waits*, describes waiting as the "spiritual art of cocooning" (page 13). She states, "Spirit needs a container to pour itself into. Grace needs an arena in which to incarnate."

What changes do you need to make in your life to allow yourself to be an empty container, to create space for God's grace to work in you?

5. Living with paradox and mystery requires us to let go of our black-and-white thinking and to live with shades of gray. Are you able to "live the questions" in your life? How comfortable are you with living the paradox of good and evil, the known and the unknown, *chronos* time and *kairos* time, control and letting go, independence and dependence? (See pages 84–89, *In the Shadow of God's Wings*.)

6. We have defined creativity far too narrowly in our culture. Julia Cameron's book *The Artist's Way: A Spiritual Path to Higher Creativity* helps open pathways in your consciousness so that creative forces can operate. Cameron states, "I have seen blocks dissolved and lives transformed by the simple process of engaging the Great Creator in discovering and recovering our creative powers" (page xi, Introduction).

The creation stories in the Bible show God's bringing forth creation out of chaos and out of a dark void. Recall times of turmoil or chaos in your life. How do you understand God to be at work in your life to recreate or to bring new life and understanding to your situation?

7. "Hope is grounded in the steadfastness of God who has acted in our past, is acting in our present, and will continue to act in our future" (page 96, *In the Shadow of God's Wings*).

Form four smaller groups and designate a recorder for each group. Assign each group one of the following scripture passages:

- Hebrews 6:13-20
- Romans 5:1-11
- Romans 8:18-30
- Romans 12 9-12

Allow ten minutes of small group discussion and preparation for a report to the whole group. The focus of this reporting centers around the question: How does this scripture reading speak to you of hope?

LOOKING AHEAD

Ask the group to read chapter 5 of *In the Shadow of God's Wings*. Remind them that next week will be the last session. Ask each participant to bring an object to next week's session that symbolizes his or her learnings, growth, or hope for the future.

CLOSING

Ask the group members to stand in a circle without holding hands. Instruct them to take one small step forward and then one small step back. Then direct them to turn their right foot at a slight angle. Have them take a small step in the direction their ankle is pointed. They will end up in a different place. Include persons with handicapping conditions in the circle, encouraging them to follow directions through movement in their chair.

Tell participants that a small step in a different direction takes us to a different place. Change is a series of small steps, and the beginning is also an ending. You may want to read the following quotation by the Indian poet, Rabindranath Tagore, taken from his work *Gitanjali (Song Offerings)*: "When old words die out on the tongue, new melodies break forth from the heart; and where the old tracks are lost, new country is revealed with its wonders." Change offers new beginnings, new possibilities, and renewed hope in the future.

Remind participants to extinguish their candles after the closing prayer and to take the candles with them as a reminder of God's presence in all the times of their lives.

You may close by praying the following prayer found on page 97 of *In the Shadow of God's Wings*.

Coming Home

O God, the journey has been so long.
I've taken every side road along the way.
I've explored all the hidden places.
As your prodigal daughter,
I've felt that I could find the way myself.

Even so, You, as loving parent, were beside me
*   picking me up when I fell*
*   sustaining me when my strength was gone*
*   nurturing me when I was helpless.*

And when I was exhausted
                     floundering
                          ready to give up,
You touched me with Your grace,
And I felt Your abundant love.

We walked back home together…
      hand in hand.

As an alternate closing, read John 1:1-5 as a benediction.

Session 4

From Disconnection to Integration

⌒

Read chapter 5 of *In the Shadow of God's Wings.*

SESSION OBJECTIVES

- To explore ways to reconnect with our authentic self
- To understand why healing can be threatening to family members and friends

SESSION MATERIALS

- Extra copies of discussion questions
- Small table and candle for worship center
- Box of tissue
- Several Bibles for the group members to share

OPENING

After lighting the candle, give those who wish the opportunity to share their objects and the reasons they symbolize their life at this time. After sharing, invite each person to place the object on the worship center.

QUESTIONS FOR GROUP DISCUSSION

1. Depressed persons often feel disconnected from their authentic, God-given self. This disconnection often has been described as a battle among different parts of ourselves.

What spiritual disciplines might help us reconnect with our whole or authentic selves?

2. As the depressed person emerges from the shadow, family and friends can experience a time of change again as the person becomes more able to care for himself or herself and becomes more assertive in stating needs. This time of emergence is a time of learning and practicing new behaviors. These new-found behaviors may disorient not only the individual but also those who love and care for the depressed person.

Share a time when you have made changes in your life. (Examples would include losing weight, giving up alcohol or nicotine, etc.) How did others react to your change?

3. Jesus asks Bartimaeus (Mark 10:46-52), "What do you want me to do for you?" (Refer to pages 99–103, *In The Shadow of God's Wings.*)

How would you respond to Jesus' question? Do you want to be healed? What changes do you expect if you are healed?

4. Many of us have a hard time saying no. Yet setting healthy boundaries is essential to physical, spiritual, and mental health.

What obstacles do you need to overcome or what changes do you need to make in order to take better care of yourself? How do you handle feelings of guilt that may arise when you cannot always meet others' expectations?

5. "Ritual puts us back into life itself; it reconnects us. The holy becomes manifest in the sacred ordinary of daily life. Rituals enable us to make transitions in our lives" (page 110, *In the Shadow of God's Wings*).

How has ritual, both public and private, helped you reconnect to the holy in your life?

LOOKING AHEAD

Though this study is ending, group members are embarking on a new beginning. They come away from the study more understanding and accepting of those persons struggling with depressive illnesses in their family, their place of work, and their place of worship. The new knowledge about mood disorders can help erase the stigma and the shame associated with this illness. They may be gentler with themselves. They can share their learnings with others and enable them to find medical, psychological, social, and spiritual help. They can help establish caring communities where an individual with this illness can find acceptance and be nurtured into the fullness God intends for all God's children. They can make a difference!

CLOSING

You may close by praying the following prayer found on page116 of *In the Shadow of God's Wings*.

> *Spirit God, you know our needs*
> > *our wounds*
> > *our hurts*
> > *our fears*
> *even before we can form them*
> *into words of prayer.*

You are patient with us.
You are protective of us.
You are present with us
    until such time that we are able
    to ask for what we need.
Thank you, Spirit God,
    for your healing taking place within
    before we are even aware
    of how broken we have become.

Materials
for
Group
Distribution

~~~~~~

Leaders may copy the following material
for student use.

What Is Depression?

MENTAL ILLNESS AFFECTS ONE IN FOUR American families each year. The "common cold" of mental illness is depression. Depression is a common, diagnosable, and treatable illness. Yet most people do not receive the treatment available either because of ignorance about the illness or because of the stigma and shame often associated with depression.

Depression is a catch-all term for feelings that range from normal times of "feeling blue" to serious clinical depression. Depressive and manic-depressive illnesses are also referred to as mood disorders or affective disorders. The term *unipolar* is often used for depression, and *bipolar* for manic depression. *Dysthymia* may refer either to a chronic, moderate depression or seasonal depression. In any given year, about eighteen million American adults have some form of affective disorder.

Statistics report that women are twice as likely as men to experience major depression. But these statistics may not accurately reflect the gender of persons who suffer from depression simply because women are more likely than men to seek help. Men and women often use addictions such as alcoholism, drug use, workaholism, overeating, and other addictive behaviors to self-medicate the emotional pain of mood disorders.

While the scientific world does not fully understand the cause of mood disorders, clearly genetic, biochemical, and environmental factors play a role. Unfortunately, according to the National Depressive and Manic-Depressive Association, two out of three people with mood disorders do not receive proper treatment because they do not recognize their symptoms; they blame the symptoms on personal weakness, or their symptoms are misdiagnosed.

The information for this section was compiled from literature for public distribution by the National Depressive and Manic-Depressive Association, the National Institute of Mental Health, the National Alliance for the Mentally Ill (NAMI), and other resources as listed in the section "Resources for People with Depression" (see page 63).

TYPES AND SYMPTOMS OF MOOD DISORDERS

Major depression or unipolar depression is characterized by the following symptoms:

- Persistent sad, depressed, or "empty" mood

- Feelings of hopelessness, pessimism

- Feelings of guilt, helplessness, worthlessness

- Decreased energy, fatigue, being "slowed down"

- Sleep disturbances, such as insomnia, early morning awakening or oversleeping

- Eating disturbances, including loss or increase in appetite

- Diminished ability to think, concentrate, or make decisions

- Loss of interest or pleasure in hobbies and activities that you once enjoyed, including sex

- Restlessness, irritability

- Persistent symptoms that do not respond to treatment, such as headaches, digestive disorders, and chronic pain

- Thoughts of death or suicide

Bipolar depression or manic-depressive illness is characterized by cycles of both depression and mania. Symptoms of mania may include the following:

- Inappropriate elation
- Inappropriate irritability
- Severe insomnia
- Grandiose notions
- Increased talking
- Disconnected and racing thoughts
- Increased sexual desire
- Markedly increased energy
- Poor judgment
- Inappropriate social behavior

Dysthymia is a low-grade, long-term depression that can go on for years. The word *dys* means "disorder" and *thymia* relates to mood. Some people have this mood disorder for most of their lives. Dysthymia does not keep persons from functioning, but its symptoms keep persons from feeling fully energetic or good.

Other kinds of depression include Seasonal Affective Disorder (SAD), postpartum depression, postoperative depression (especially with major surgery), and depression arising from chronic pain.

Frequently Used Medications

F OR DEPRESSION, YOUR DOCTOR MAY PRESCRIBE medications known collectively as antidepressants. The older lines of antidepressants include tricyclics and monoamine oxidase inhibitors.

While many classes of antidepressants are available, research has showed that none of the antidepressants is more effective or works more quickly than the others. They all take several weeks to become effective. The difference among the classes is in the side effects and dosage.

*   *Tricyclic Antidepressants*
    Janimine, Tofranil(Imipramine)
    Elavil (Amitriptyline)
    Adapin (Doxepin)
    Pamelor (Nortriptyline)

*   *Monoamine Oxidase Inhibitors (MAOIs)*
    Nardil (Phenelzine)
    Parnate (Tranylcypromine)

A second generation of cyclics was developed later to help those who did not respond well to the older drugs.

- *Atypical Medications*
  Desyrel (Trazodone)
  Wellbutrin (Bupropion Hydrochloride)

  During the past several years, the selective serotonin reuptake inhibitors (SSRIs) have become the first-line treatment for depression, as they generally act on a more specific neurotransmitter in the brain. They have fewer side effects than tricyclics.

- *Selective Serotonin Reuptake Inhibitors (SSRIs)*
  Prozac (Fluoxetine Hydrochloride)
  Zoloft (Sertraline Hydrochloride)
  Paxil (Paroxetine)
  Luvox (Fluvoxamine Maleate)

  More recently, the selective serotonin noradrenergic reuptake inhibitors (SSNRIs) have come into use.

- *Selective Serotonin Noradrenergic Reuptake Inhibitors (SSNRIs)*
  Effexor (Venlafaxine)
  Serzone (Nefazodone)

  Compared to the available treatments for depression, there are fewer medications to treat bipolar disorder. Physicians often prescribe antidepressants for episodes of depression in people with manic-depressive illness, while treating the manic phase with mood stabilizers.

- *Mood Stabilizers for Bipolar Depression*
  Lithium Carbonate, Eskalith (Lithium)
  Depakote, Depakene (Valproic acid, sodium valproate)
  Tegretol˚ (Carbamazepine)

IN ADDITION TO THE ABOVE MEDICATIONS, supplemental treatment of mood disorders can include other classes of medications such as the following:

- *Benzodiazepines*
  Klonopin (Clonazepam)
  Ativan (Lorazepam)

- *Neuroleptics*
  Risperdal (Risperidone)
  Mellaril, Thorazine (Chlorpromazine)

- *Thyroid Hormone Replacements*

Medications have proved to be highly effective in treating mood disorders, but many people refuse to take medication. Some fear that a drug will change their basic personality, sedate them into a zombie-like state, or cause them to become drug dependent. While many drugs can cause side effects, the benefits far outweigh any problems.

Your doctor will discover that one class of medication is more effective than another for your type of depression, and he or she will choose a drug within that class that proves to have the lowest side-effect profile for you. Not everyone has the same reaction to one drug, so it may take some time to discover the most effective and most comfortable medication for you.

One of the most difficult issues a person with a depressive illness may face is the length of time before a medication begins to work. In cases of depression, a given medication can take two to three weeks to reduce symptoms and several weeks longer to achieve complete relief. Unfortunately side effects appear earlier in treatment than the wanted antidepressant effects. Most side effects resolve with time.

~ 49 ~

From In the Shadow of God's Wings Study Guide © *1998 by Susan Gregg-Schroeder.*
Permission to copy granted to purchaser by Upper Room Books.

The slowness of efficacy with early side effects can sorely try a person with depressive illness, who wonders when or if treatment will help. During this period, the help and support of family, friends, mental health professionals, the church community, and others is crucial for bolstering one's motivation to continue the prescribed medications.

* Data is incomplete on Tegretol as a second or third medication choice after Lithium for persons with bipolar disorder. Despite this, Tegretol, an anticonvulsant, has been prescribed with success since the 1970s for treatment of manic depressives who cannot tolerate Lithium.

Other Treatment Options

ELECTROCONVULSIVE THERAPY (ECT)

Some persons who have been severely depressed over a long period of time are unable to take antidepressants due to heart conditions, old age, or other physical factors. For them, electroconvulsive therapy may be the best treatment option. For others, medication and psychotherapy fail to adequately alleviate severe depression, and the doctor may recommend electroconvulsive therapy. ECT is a safe and effective treatment. Since its early use in the 1930s, ECT has been refined and improved. Unfortunately, stigmatizing images prevent some people from considering it as an option.

ECT works through a mild electrical stimulation of the brain. It is not fully understood how this treatment affects the biochemical imbalance in the brain. This electrical stimulation causes short, modified seizures. The patient receives muscle relaxants and anesthesia before ECT to protect him or her from harm. An average of six to twelve treatments over a three- to four-week period is required. Medication or infrequent "maintenance" treatments of ECT often can control subsequent episodes of depression.

PSYCHOTHERAPY

While medication is often essential to treat the chemical changes in the brain, psychotherapy—or "talk therapy"— is an important part of most patients' treatment. Talk therapy may be the sole treatment in cases of mild to moderate depres-

From In the Shadow of God's Wings Study Guide © *1998 by Susan Gregg-Schroeder.*
Permission to copy granted to purchaser by Upper Room Books.

sion. Severe depression or mania may require another form of treatment prior to psychotherapy.

Three types of psychotherapy have proved effective in reducing symptoms:

1. Psychodynamic therapies concentrate on resolving internal psychological conflicts, often rooted in childhood.

2. Cognitive/behavioral therapy focuses on changing negative or self-destructive thoughts and beliefs in order to change behavior patterns.

3. Interpersonal therapy focuses on current relationships.

Selecting a Doctor or Therapist

S ELECTING THE RIGHT DOCTOR or therapist is key to successful management of a mood disorder. Choose someone with whom you can be open and forthright. Other important factors in choosing a professional include selecting a doctor or therapist who respects your value system, who is willing to treat "the whole person," and who is willing to work with your family and friends.

Only a medical doctor can prescribe medications. If medications are recommended, be sure your physician is competent in the management of psychiatric medications. Sometimes your family doctor is not the best person to provide this care. In that case, you might find a psychiatrist, a medical doctor trained in the study of both psychotherapy and medication management.

For either individual or group psychotherapy, you may choose a psychologist or a pastoral counselor. Pastoral counselors are clergy—pastors, priests, rabbis—who are also mental health professionals. As such, they are trained in two disciplines: psychology and theology. A pastoral counselor may be the answer for individuals desiring both a mental health professional and someone who is also sensitive to religious and spiritual matters. The American Association of Pastoral Counselors will recommend the name of a certified pastoral counselor near you.

Food Affects Mood

⌒

D URING THE PAST TWO DECADES, hundreds of studies have identified tangible effects that certain foods have on our brain chemistry. The leader of this food and mood movement is Dr. Judith Wurtman, a nutrition researcher at Massachusetts Institute of Technology (MIT). Dr. Wurtman states, "We've found that some foods influence brain chemicals involved in determining mood, mental energy, performance and behavior."

Wurtman has written extensively, outlining the results of studies of how food affects brain chemistry. Some foods cited in various studies show that eating whole grain bread helps boost the amino acid tryptophan, which acts to elevate the levels of serotonin in the brain—similar to the serotonin reuptake inhibitors in certain antidepressant medications. Chocolate also appears to boost levels of serotonin—good news for chocolate lovers! Turkey has been shown to boost levels of the brain chemicals dopamine and norepinephrine, which results in more energy and reduced stress. Bananas are important for their magnesium, which increases immunity and energy. Citrus fruits, while one of the best sources of vitamin C, also boost levels of the brain chemical norepinephrine, a neurotransmitter that regulates alertness, attentiveness, and motivation.

While one should not ignore the extreme symptoms of depression and other mood disorders when medical attention is appropriate, making a few simple dietary changes may help us all feel better. What we eat affects our memory, mood, and vitality as well as our overall physical health and our risk of disease.

Depression in Different Age Groups

CHILDHOOD DEPRESSION

Estimates of the National Institute of Mental Health indicate that close to 7.5 percent of children in the United States suffer from depression. Childhood depressive symptoms don't resemble those of depression in adults. Thus, depression in children is not easily recognized. The symptoms of childhood depression can include:

- Unexplained and frequent stomachaches, headaches, or fatigue
- Excessive restlessness or sluggishness
- Excessive worrying
- Significant change in weight
- Noticeably different sleep patterns
- Excessive, unprovoked hostility or aggression
- Lack of interest in playing and interactivity

TEENAGE DEPRESSION

The third leading cause of death for teenagers is suicide. These are difficult years as teens struggle to find their own identity. Sometimes life's problems can cause a teenager to feel overwhelmed and can trigger depression. Parents' divorce, death of a loved one, a break up with a girlfriend or boyfriend, poor grades: All these factors increase the pressure. While many teens find ways to cope with these pressures, others become depressed and may need treatment.

Some of the signs and symptoms of teenage depression are these:

- Difficulty achieving in school
- Constant anger
- Rebellious acts
- Trouble with family, friends, and peers
- Excessive alcohol and/or drug use
- Low self-esteem or self-worth
- Suicidal thoughts and attempts

DEPRESSION IN OLDER ADULTS

Depression can be a common and significant problem in the elderly and long-term care patients. Depressive symptoms occur in over 5 million (16 percent) of the estimated 33 million Americans over the age of 65. Studies report that one in four nursing home residents may suffer from depression. Studies show that approximately one-fourth of older adults with a significant medical illness also may be depressed.

Diagnosing depression in the elderly can be complicated. Certain medications, such as those used in the treatment of hypertension, Parkinson's disease, sleep disorders, or pain may raise the risk of depression in the elderly. It is important to communicate all health information to a doctor.

Some signs of depression, such as memory lapses and difficulty in concentration, can mimic Alzheimer's disease or other medical disorders. For a proper diagnosis and to rule out other disorders, schedule a thorough medical examination. A person can have depression and another illness such as Alzheimer's disease at the same time. Even in such a case, treating the depression can relieve unnecessary suffering.

Older adults, when depressed, often speak of physical symptoms rather than feelings of being anxious, tired, or sad. Caregivers and family members may need to advocate for the elderly person. With proper treatment, the elderly or long-term care patient can live a more fulfilling and happier life.

Coping Strategies for the Family

W HEN A FAMILY MEMBER IS SUFFERING with a depressive illness, it affects the whole family just as any illness. Supportive relationships with family members, including spouses, is key to the day-to-day management of mood disorders.

Some coping strategies for family members include the following:

- Have realistic expectations; do not think that you can "cure" the depression.

- Provide unconditional love and support to the family member experiencing depression.

- Maintain your daily routine as much as possible.

- Talk about your feelings.

- Don't take the depressed person's symptoms and reactions personally.

- Allow yourself to get help when you need it.

From In the Shadow of God's Wings Study Guide © *1998 by Susan Gregg-Schroeder. Permission to copy granted to purchaser by Upper Room Books.*

Resources for Persons with Depression

T HE FOLLOWING SOURCES OFFER INFORMATION and/or support organizations that have local offices throughout the country. Write or call for a listing of how to contact these groups in your community.

American Association of Pastoral Counselors
9504A Lee Hwy
Fairfax, VA 22031-2303
(703) 385-6967

American Psychiatric Association
1400 K St., NW
Washington, D.C. 20005
(800) 368-5777; (202) 682-6000

The Carter Center Mental Health Program
One Copenhill
453 Freedom Parkway
Atlanta, GA 30307
(404) 420-5165

D/ART (DEPRESSION / Awareness, Recognition, Treatment)
National Institute of Mental Health
5600 Fishers Lane
Rockville, MD 20857
(800) 421-4211

Depression and Related Affective Disorders Association
Johns Hopkins Hospital Meyer 3-181
600 N. Wolfe St.

Baltimore, MD 21287-7381
(410) 955-4647; (202) 955-5800
Fax: (410) 614-3241

NAMI (National Alliance for the Mentally Ill)
200 N. Glebe Rd., Suite 1015
Arlington, VA 22203-3754
(800) 950-NAMI; FAX: (703) 524-9094

NAFDI (National Foundation for Depressive Illness)
P.O. Box 2257
New York, NY 10116
(212) 268-4260; FAX: (212) 268-4434

NDMDA (National Depressive and Manic-Depressive Association)
730 North Franklin St., Suite 501
Chicago, IL 60610
(800) 826-3632; (312) 642-0049
FAX: (312) 642-7243

NIMH (National Institute of Mental Health)
5600 Fishers Lane
Rockville, MD 20857
(301) 443-4513

National Mental Health Association
1021 Prince Street
Alexandria, VA 22314-2971
(703) 684-7722; FAX: (703) 684-5968

WFMH (World Federation for Mental Health)
1021 Prince St.
Alexandria, VA 22314
(703) 838-7543
FAX: (703) 519-7648

Session 1 Study Guide
Understanding Depression

B efore the first session, read the Prologue and chapter 1 of
In the Shadow of God's Wings.

QUESTIONS FOR GROUP REFLECTION

1. "Story has great power, transforming power. Part of that
transforming power comes from the intimacy of storytelling.
The stories of our faith heritage, the stories of others, and our
own stories make up the fabric of our soul" (page 11, *In the
Shadow of God's Wings*).

When have hearing another's story or sharing your own
story "become windows through which we look at the experiences that have shaped our lives and the lives of others"? (page
11, *In the Shadow of God's Wings*)

2. What happens when we keep family secrets, when we do
not share our stories because of shame, guilt, or fear of others'
reactions?

3. What words or images come to mind when you think of the
word *shadow*?

4. Recall a time in your life, past or present, when you have
entered into deep darkness or the "valley of the shadow of
death." How did you feel? How did others feel toward you?

LOOKING AHEAD

Read chapters 2 and 3 of *In the Shadow of God's Wings*. Consider keeping a journal or writing notes on the study questions for these four weeks. Practice the discipline of journaling by recording your thoughts, feelings, struggles, hopes, and other issues prompted by group discussion or by reading the book. For those inexperienced with journaling, some possible journal entries might include the following:

* Insights or questions arising from your reading

* Quotations from the book that have personal significance

* Reflections on how ideas in the book relate to your personal experience

* Thoughts, ideas or questions that come up during group discussion

CLOSING

You may close by praying the following prayer found on pages 54–55 of *In the Shadow of God's Wings*.

> *Here I am, Divine Spirit,*
> *   living in the center of mystery.*
> *I catch glimpses of brilliant light*
> *   breaking in all around.*
> *Yet I am attracted to the darkness*
> *   that shields me*
> *   that hides me*
> *   that keeps me safe.*
> *I feel yearnings to birth*
> *   the creative spirit within.*
> *Yet I fear the changes*
> *   that new life will bring.*

It's hard to understand this place,
    this center of mystery.
The light and dark intermingle.
Life and death abide side by side.
It is here that I live the questions
        in my soul,
    knowing that one day
    answers to those questions
    will be birthed
    from this center of mystery.

From In the Shadow of God's Wings Study Guide © 1998 by Susan Gregg-Schroeder.
Permission to copy granted to purchaser by Upper Room Books.

Session 2 Study Guide
Caring for the Depressed Person

$\diagdown$

Read chapters 2 and 3 of *In the Shadow of God's Wings*.

QUESTIONS FOR REFLECTION

1. Western society often views suffering as the opposite of health. Westerners are strongly influenced by a form of early Christianity that saw evil in suffering. This form of Christianity understood suffering as shameful, something to be endured alone. Particularly before the nineteenth century many Christians viewed suffering as punishment from God. Thus our society has come to value strength, health, and self-sufficiency. Fortunately, this view of suffering is giving way to a more wholistic attitude. But many people still feel personally responsible for their suffering.

Why do you feel that people suffer?

2. The book relates the journey through depression as similar to experiencing the stages in the grief process: denial, isolation, anger, bargaining, depression and acceptance.

As you recall your times of deep pain or depression, how do you identify with this process?

3. Depression affects relationship dynamics within the family and among friends. Often the caregiver becomes the one in need of care from others.

~ 69 ~

How does it feel to be in need of help? Are you able to ask for help from others in your times of physical, emotional, or psychological need? If not, what holds you back from asking for help?

4. When persons experience depression, they are often very hard on themselves for not being able to "snap out of it."

What might family and friends say or do that would be hurtful to someone who is depressed? In what ways can family and friends be helpful?

5. We are often quick to judge another's behavior when we have not been there ourselves. Parker J. Palmer, in his book *The Active Life* writes, "In the midst of my depression I had a friend who took a different tack. Every afternoon at around four o'clock he came to me, sat in a chair, removed my shoes, and massaged my feet. He hardly said a word, but he was there, he was with me. He was a lifeline for me, a link to the human community and thus to my own humanity. He had no need to 'fix' me. He knew the meaning of compassion."

Knowing more about the illness of depression, how might you respond to a person suffering with depression?

6. The book relates the story of Elijah's experience with depression (pages 40–42, *In the Shadow of God's Wings;* and see 1 Kings 18–19). What does this story say about ways the faith community could respond to persons suffering with depression?

7. The story is told of discovering the bumper sticker with the words *Grace Happens* (page 49, *In the Shadow of God's Wings*). As you reflect on your life, when has God's grace surprised you?

LOOKING AHEAD

Read chapter 4 of *In the Shadow of God's Wings*. You are encouraged to keep writing in your journals and recording any thoughts or feelings that come up in your reading or from the class discussion.

You may close by praying the following prayer found on page 47 of *In the Shadow of God's Wings*.

> *Break into my confusion, God.*
> *Help me to know who I am*
> *and what I am meant to be.*
>
> *Guide, uphold, and strengthen me,*
> *as I leave behind*
> *the world of limits and labels.*
>
> *Guide, uphold and strengthen me,*
> *as together we create*
> *a world of infinite possibility.*

Session 3 Study Guide
Discovering the Spiritual Gifts of Depression

⟨～⟩

Read chapter 4 of *In the Shadow of God's Wings.*

QUESTIONS FOR REFLECTION

1. A time of crisis can be an opportunity for personal and spiritual growth. Thomas Moore states in his book *Care of the Soul*, "If we persist in our modern way of treating depression as an illness to be cured only mechanically and chemically we may lose the gifts of soul that only depression can provide" (pages 59–60, *In the Shadow of God's Wings*).

Reflect on a difficult time in your life. What "gifts" did you receive from going through that time of darkness and sadness?

2. Henri J. M. Nouwen has written in his book *The Wounded Healer*, "A Christian community is therefore a healing community not because wounds are cured and pains are alleviated, but because wounds and pains become openings or occasions for a new vision" (page 94).

In the Shadow of God's Wings discusses three aspects of the gift of vulnerability: vulnerability to God, vulnerability to ourselves, and vulnerability to community. In what ways might our wounds become signs of hope and "occasions for a new vision" when we take a risk and share them?

3. Discovering the gift of one's authentic self requires discovering who you are as a child of God. This discovery can be a lifelong process. What are some ways that you honor yourself so as to discover the treasure hidden in the field of your soul?

4. A Russian proverb says, "The future belongs to those who know how to wait." Waiting can be a time of emptiness. Sue Monk Kidd, in her book *When the Heart Waits*, describes waiting as the "spiritual art of cocooning" (page 13). She states, "Spirit needs a container to pour itself into. Grace needs an arena in which to incarnate."

What changes do you need to make in your life to allow yourself to be an empty container, to create space for God's grace to work in you?

5. Living with paradox and mystery requires us to let go of our black-and-white thinking and to live with shades of gray. Are you able to "live the questions" in your life? How comfortable are you with living the paradox of good and evil, the known and the unknown, *chronos* time and *kairos* time, control and letting go, independence and dependence? (See pages 84–89, *In the Shadow of God's Wings*.)

6. We have defined creativity far too narrowly in our culture. Julia Cameron's book *The Artist's Way: A Spiritual Path to Higher Creativity* helps open pathways in your consciousness so that creative forces can operate. Cameron states, "I have seen blocks dissolved and lives transformed by the simple process of engaging the Great Creator in discovering and recovering our creative powers" (page xi, Introduction).

The creation stories in the Bible show God's bringing forth creation out of chaos and out of a dark void. Recall times of turmoil or chaos in your life. How do you understand God to be at work in your life to recreate or to bring new life and understanding to your situation?

7. "Hope is grounded in the steadfastness of God who has acted in our past, is acting in our present, and will continue to act in our future" (page 96, *In the Shadow of God's Wings*).

Read the following scripture passages:

- Hebrews 6:13-20
- Romans 5:1-11
- Romans 8: 18-30
- Romans 12: 9-12

How do these scripture readings speak to you of hope?

LOOKING AHEAD

Read chapter 5 of *In the Shadow of God's Wings*. Next week will be the last session. Please bring an object to next week's session that symbolizes your learnings, growth, or hope for the future.

CLOSING

You may close by praying the following prayer found on page 97 of *In the Shadow of God's Wings*.

Coming Home

O God, the journey has been so long.
I've taken every side road along the way.
I've explored all the hidden places.
As your prodigal daughter,
I've felt that I could find the way myself.

From *In the Shadow of God's Wings Study Guide* © *1998 by Susan Gregg-Schroeder. Permission to copy granted to purchaser by Upper Room Books.*

Even so, You, as loving parent, were beside me
picking me up when I fell
sustaining me when my strength was gone
nurturing me when I was helpless.
And when I was exhausted
floundering
ready to give up,
You touched me with Your grace,
And I felt Your abundant love.

We walked back home together…
hand in hand.

As an alternate closing, read John 1:1-5 as a benediction.

Session 4 Study Guide
From Disconnection
to Integration

R ead chapter 5 of *In the Shadow of God's Wings.*

QUESTIONS FOR REFLECTION

1. Depressed persons often feel disconnected from their authentic, God-given self. This disconnection often has been described as a battle among different parts of ourselves.

What spiritual disciplines might help us reconnect with our whole or authentic selves?

2. As the depressed person emerges from the shadow, family and friends can experience a time of change again as the person becomes more able to care for himself or herself and becomes more assertive in stating needs. This time of emergence is a time of learning and practicing new behaviors. These new-found behaviors may disorient not only the individual but also those who love and care for the depressed person.

Think of a time when you have made changes in your life. (Examples would include losing weight, giving up alcohol or nicotine, etc.) How did others react to your change?

3. Jesus asks Bartimaeus (Mark 10:46-52), "What do you want

me to do for you?" (Refer to pages 99–103, *In The Shadow of God's Wings.*)

How would you respond to Jesus' question? Do you want to be healed? What changes do you expect if you are healed?

4. Many of us have a hard time saying no. Yet setting healthy boundaries is essential to physical, spiritual, and mental health.

What obstacles do you need to overcome or what changes do you need to make in order to take better care of yourself? How do you handle feelings of guilt that may arise when you cannot always meet others' expectations?

5. "Ritual puts us back into life itself; it reconnects us. The holy becomes manifest in the sacred ordinary of daily life. Rituals enable us to make transitions in our lives" (page 110, *In the Shadow of God's Wings*).

How has ritual, both public and private, helped you reconnect to the holy in your life?

LOOKING AHEAD

While this study is ending, you are embarking on a new beginning. You come away from the study more understanding and accepting of those persons struggling with depressive illnesses in your family, your place of work, and your place of worship. Your new knowledge about mood disorders can help erase the stigma and the shame associated with this illness. You may be gentler with yourself. You can share your learnings with others and enable them to find medical, psychological, social, and spiritual help. You can help establish caring communities where an individual with this illness can be accepted and nurtured into the fullness God intends for all God's children. You can make a difference!

CLOSING

You may close by praying the following prayer found on page 116 of *In the Shadow of God's Wings*.

> *Spirit God, you know our needs*
> > *our wounds*
> > *our hurts*
> > *our fears*
> > *even before we can form them*
> > *into words of prayer.*
> *You are patient with us.*
> *You are protective of us.*
> *You are present with us*
> > *until such time that we are able*
> > *to ask for what we need.*
> *Thank you, Spirit God,*
> > *for your healing taking place within*
> > *before we are even aware*
> > *of how broken we have become.*

About the Author

Susan Gregg-Schroeder lives in San Diego, California, where she serves as one of the pastors of First United Methodist Church of San Diego. Her articles and poetry have appeared in *The Christian Ministry*, *Faith at Work*, *Church Worship*, and *Alive Now*. She is the author of four other books, including *For Your Hospital Visit: Prayers and Meditations for Children*, published by The Upper Room.